"*I'll Leave a Light On for You* is an absolutely luminous meditation on what it means to love in a world where nothing can be held forever. Bortz has a way of holding space for the grief of what cannot last while reminding us why it's worth it. Here, love is fleeting—and still everything."

— **ELISE M. POWERS**
Author of *The Size of Your Joy*

"Tender, lyrical, and achingly gorgeous, in *I'll Leave a Light On for You*, poet William Bortz devotedly turns toward the people he loves—his wife, his daughter—and the ordinary moments of his life where beauty lives. With breathtaking intimacy, he speaks of them as if the whole world begins and ends in their hands. Woven through it all is the nostalgic pain of his own childhood and relationship with his father, alongside the gentle, luminous devotion towards the daughter that made him one."

— **ROSE BRIK**
Author of *my father's eyes, my mother's rage*

Praise for *The Grief We're Given*

"A luminous and consistently breathtaking exploration of grief, Bortz's stunningly crafted writing will stay with you long after its final exhale."

— **BLAKE AUDEN**
Author of *Murmuration*

"With their quiet intensity and graceful questioning, these verses will pull you inside yourself and out into mysterious communal joy."

— **CHRISTINE JEWEL**
Author of *Fading Through*

I'll Leave a Light On for You

- poems -

william bortz

Published by Central Avenue Poetry, an imprint of Central Avenue Marketing Ltd.
centralavenuepublishing.com

I'LL LEAVE A LIGHT ON FOR YOU: Poems

Trade Paperback: 978-1-77168-457-6
Ebook: 978-1-77168-458-3

Printed in the United States of America

1. POETRY / Love 2. POETRY / Family

1 3 5 7 9 10 8 6 4 2

For Ella

For Chelsie

CONTENTS

VIEW FROM MY THERAPIST'S WINDOW

THE SEARCHLIGHTS SPIN

I'll leave a light on for you
—Chelsie

View from my therapist's window

I often go back to the past and wait for a light to flicker on
—but one never does

Battalion of joy

One day these sweet things will
unfurl into something intangible,

but today they are here—
this pair of shadows, this battalion of joy.

Two hands from two bodies placed
on top of one another creates a home.

In this home, we leave small holes in the roof,
we let the sun in, we let the rain trickle in.

There will come a day when these things we're holding
can't be held any longer,

but today we lock the door because we are busy—
we drink the rain, we lie in the sunbeams.

I see nothing, I hear nothing
but your shadow, but your body.

It's possible all we have is this moment

though I can't be sure because I continue
to dream about the next, and they're quite vibrant.
I will grasp onto you just in case.

The day I ran away

I believed freedom	was a place	one could
arrive at	my hands were	as soft as
the underbelly of a	tulip	and I remember
that felt a lot	like failing	this body is meant
to break	I am a sky	undone by noise
if I keep running	I will no longer	have a name
the only home	I know is away	from here
the only price	to be paid for	leaving is
memory	and in those	photographs
I am still the	small child	you never
stopped	carrying gently	to bed
this body is	meant to break	and from
its shell	light will	pour out

I could be different

stronger, if I tried,

allow the rain to drip slowly off me, gentler

or slower. I could go beyond the

remembering—it lives somewhere

between holding and letting

go. You told me to love

and I thought that just meant

you, but now in this moment

I know you meant

everything.

Somewhere in West Virginia

I only ever spoke with my father one time before he died / what that means is my whole life is a lesson I wasn't prepared to learn / what I mean is in all my memories your face turns to smoke / whenever I see something gentler than gentle / a doe, a single small cloud in a vast and endless sky, a toddler holding a fruit / I can feel the ways in which I am split / severed / part bent wire frame containing overgrowth / part overgrowth pushing the frame outward, nearly bursting / what I mean is on any given day I am capable of dismantling / either because there is so much softness left to witness / or because I was once a softness / and can't remember being held / by someone who didn't want me to rupture

I am from this country

I have always lived within its walls.

Watched those outside its walls.

Have seen those outside its walls die.

Held the last breath of some inside its walls.

I have always been told it is safe here.

Grasping

My daughter's first act of love
was wrapping her fingers
around one of mine and holding on
after grabbing at everything else
and letting go.

The unrivaled burden of memory

yes, I do remember the rivers in your palm & how mostly you filled them with the crushed dust of small, pale, chalky fruits & by fruit I of course mean a sweetness so good it could only be natural & by natural I mean there was no option or outcome other than believing this dust could turn you into smoke & I did often watch through the keyhole of the door as you worshipped a reality that you favored much more & yes, this reality was one in which you were a fonder memory & you didn't notice the record skipping & in my memory it sounds like the quick crack of thunder & specifically the kind that is so close you cover your head once the sound echoes as if that would actually protect you & by you I mean mother & by protect I mean you came into this world screaming & no one even tried gently rocking you or calming you down with a loving voice & I wish I had opened the door in order to try but I didn't know how

Who am I? and other impossible questions

Spending much of my life fragile,
I wanted to undo the thing
I never asked to be done.
My father's hand gripped tightly
around my frail-bird wrist,
forever leading me to someplace
I did not want to go.

We can't afford to do anything so we go to Lowe's so you can daydream about what flowers you would plant on our balcony

Maybe pansies. For sure something that won't attract more wasps.
Those violent, fragile things—like shattered glass in a car wreck.

Ultimately, you decide on perennials. They are heartier—stronger. You say, *Whatever takes the least amount of attention and is the hardest to kill.*

Our daughter, led by her whimsy, walks toward the back of the garden section and watches a man blow the gravel out of the walkways with a leaf blower.

We become elated at the thought of buying birdseed for our Bluetooth birdfeeder—and decide not to activate the camera part of it and allow it to be a private little birdhome.

On the way home, we argue. Our daughter, in the backseat, plays with her fingers and toes. I intentionally miss our turn so we can find a resolution before the long elevator ride.

The evening sun warms the empty soil of our window boxes. A bird lands on the railing of our balcony briefly, then flies off. Our daughter watches, her mouth pressed open against

the glass. Your hand is soft against mine, like a cloud dulling the edge of a horizon as it provides shade or rain or both to someplace that is needing it, I'm sure.

Hierarchy of longing

if I give the flower a name
I have killed it

brother, where have you placed yourself
in your hierarchy of longings

the way your head tilts back
when laughter erupts in your chest

everything adored is not aware
of its own breathing

I ask God if plucked flowers go to heaven

Are they planted along the golden road,
filling the air with a heavy sweetness?

When we sing of our suffering here,
do they tilt their heads down

and remember their final act?
Transferred from moving hands to unmoving ones—

a gift of vibrancy, just a shadow of what
we were once holding,

but enough to make us sing.

Sky

would it drop me if it knew
I paint the faces of those I love
in its palm

Body

Pain has its own body
and it, too, can lie still
while moonlight slivers its
limbs into stripes—
and it, too, can miss
being held.

The bombs continue to fall

we were born of explosions
we came out covered in ash
my father was fire
we drink and are still thirsty
we decorate our walls with the bodies
we go to church
(we sit and kneel and recite their names as prayers)
we are handed another day
we say thank you
we do not consider how many times it was unsuccessfully pried from our hands
we were born of whimsy
from out the window, the faraway bombs looked like rain
we feel the phantom pain of countless losses
we rub our bodies together to prove that we still have bodies to rub together
we listen closely between fall and eruption
we hear the birds sing
we name the sound *mother*
we let our mothers hold us
we hold our mothers
we hold

White gold

When I remember
lying awake in a strange bed
in a strange house,

my mother
beneath the same moon
in a different strange house,

I imagine God
in his white gold home
listening to the same rain as me,

wondering
if the sound
of each droplet
hitting the roof

was too loud
for him to hear me
ask him to

open the door.

My answer when asked if I love my father

When I speak my name into the wind
I do not get a response

*

A drop of my blood falls into the flowing river—
it doesn't locate a current

*

I love his ghost, who passes through my hands
like walls in a house that has never been anything
but empty

*

In the same way we break slowly, tenderly, over time—
we cannot see it

*

You can have my shirt to use as a tourniquet for your wound—
or take my hands, cupped together like a bowl to catch the drops—
they should not be spilled

*

My daughter speaks the word "dada"
and the cigarette burn on my forearm
blossoms into a dandelion

The searchlights spin

Already, much of this living has been pain. I have loved for nothing and loved for everything. Given the chance, I would do it again.

Apple picking

I want this to be permanent—
your face drunk with light, tucking your hair behind your ear.

Our daughter cooing as she discovers her feet—a country.
The wind finally growing quiet and warming.

A bee lands gingerly on her arm, just below the elbow—
she watches it, smiling a small smile the size of an apple slice;

to her, everything is a magic trick—she knows nothing of danger.
She squints as she looks up, the sun licks her cheeks.

I can't believe some of this will have to be given back
and still, I must be kind.

I don't know anything

and struggle to follow a recipe.
I once added drugs to drugs and felt
nothing, still. On long drives
through flat prairie land, I listen
to old songs, but ghosts do not
flow in through the metal and glass
in order to sit beside me.
When I am happy, I drink,
but this does not make me any
happier. After my daughter goes
to sleep, I flip through pictures of
her when she was younger, smaller,
resting in the crook of my arm or
spinning in tight, clockwise circles
(dancing), and yet I am happy she
continues to grow. I remember, and
I cry. During Covid, I learned to make
French-style scrambled eggs. Gleefully,
I stirred the thick yolks in a pot,
scraping the edges, not letting them sit
still (too long). I delicately placed
them on old ceramic plates, topped
them with dill, and added cherry
tomatoes next to them, just barely
touching. My wife ate them in the
sun, quietly, while drinking coffee.
Smiling, I think she would not
have told me if they weren't any good.

We make music while the world is dismantled around us

This quiet is what we've begged for—
we have scraped and scrapped, pleaded
for it.

The reflection of dusk splintering in your eyes—
the acid clouds, the green hue of tomorrow, taking
form as a wish.

I've had my share of poisons, smokes
beneath streetlights, clear liquor out of
plastic cups.

Your hand in mine is a small bird—
I have watched it yearn—its small wings
inhaling before the first flutter.

I cut down a tree to get the highest apple;
it was sweet, but I was alone—
you would have stopped me.

Nothing can grow in the dirt
and yet, we plant—
we sing to the seed.

Our voices dripping, heavy.
I'd give any air left to this,
to belief.

We sing because we are here
from seemingly
nothing.

Gospel Mission

Not homeless, home-hopeful, home-harboring
hands that have sewn an infinity's length of quilts
pulled up to the chins of children they'll never hold.
If there could be a way to measure love, this could be it:
rooms full of couches and La-Z-Boy recliners made for
planning, made for daydreaming, but repurposed for
jungle gyms, for distractions—and how I indulged,
joining the other children in gathering all the lumpy,
sun-bleached cushions together and constructing
walls out of them, ceilings in some places, ramps in others,
building a mansion for all of us to play house in.
The mothers all sit around the kitchen table right outside the door,
quietly, watching, slicing oranges and apples onto one paper plate.
A feast we will enjoy after all our hard work.

August 8th, 2025

how do I send her to school
not knowing who will be
picking her up

Fruit

We love not ourselves
but what we want to be.
We love that we tell ourselves
we're getting close—
we love a ghost,
a tree in the distance.
From here, the fruit is almost visible,
ripe and dripping.

It is spring and I can feel again

Watch as everything once bare blossoms again.
It's almost enough to make you believe in something.
It's almost enough to make you forget everything
that left and didn't come back.

The hair that falls from the braid you tuck behind your ear

a wispy cloud I point
to and gasp—
such a delicate thing

I would sacrifice this
body to gravity
just to feel it

After I broke my wrist

I couldn't pick up my daughter for a month.
Then, she was a firework, an uncatchable thing—
a moth drawn to light only she could see.
Always following closely behind her—
ready to catch her, if needed, with my one good arm.
Always mentally doing the math of distance, considering angles.
Force, weight, velocity, etc.
And I thought, *She knows nothing of the suffering we willfully enter into.*
One day, she will break apart herself—for joy, love, or belief.
And most likely, I will be more than a footstep behind her.
Perhaps behind a door that is closed and cannot be reopened.

What is there to worry about

Summer keeps pressing its hands

into me,

and there are also your hands.

Those little birds, those

raging stars.

I wake up with their outlines

still burning on my chest.

I can't explain the state that I'm in—the state of my heart

after "The Predatory Wasp of the Palisades Is Out to Get Us!" by Sufjan Stevens

I won't ever stop tightening the rivets of my appreciation until it holds / thinking outrageously, I pierce a stale afternoon's sunbeam with the tip of my finger / with the purest blood ribbon in my hand / the state that I'm in is wonder / and everything is a fragment of something holier than I can hold / I have empty hands and a good name for everything / there is still so much of me that doubts there is an end to any river / all the small instances of brilliance simply flow slowly to coagulation / how could there be a collection of it all / a shimmering sea in constant movement / where nothing is too heavy / where nothing sinks / if I don't believe this, will every noise from an early-risen bird fail to blossom into a song / every shimmering silhouette of a tree swaying in front of a moon remains winter instead of sprouting into spring / I pull my finger from the column of light / and become a shadow

What should we call the sun

on the first warm day after a long, cold winter / stardust / the bones of my bones / that which heals when time does not / the perfect eye of my imperfect lover / you hold my face in your palms like a warm rain / god of softness / that which calls me to forget the many calamities of my life, such as / how soft a bumblebee is and yet I cannot hold it / the ghost of my father passing through the walls of my hands / the silence after the song that fills my lungs ends / that tomorrow you may be tucked into the pocket of a gray and stale afternoon / and I may forget that we met / and then I will call you / a good memory

Even when the day is over

no wars have been won
we let the fruit grow soft in its cold bowl
there were many kinder words that could've been chosen
the light wasn't left humming on the porch
no portraits were painted with this tongue
the memories recalled were sour, stinging
even when the day is over,
we are two rivers that return to the same sea

I learned late

That there are equations for measuring
how much a gust of wind can topple over.

How to properly eat a pear—just a few days ago, actually.
I thought the skin was to be avoided, thought the core inside was festering.

That if I turned off the lamp, I could see outside more clearly—
a small moon painted into the rain puddles on the driveway.

Wind remembers any part of the body it's allowed to hold.
I cannot soften light; light softens me.

That I should hold the names of those I love
in my throat like a garden.

That I will return to that garden many, many
times just to stand among what's grown there.

A different face

There have been so many versions of me
I simply cannot recall each one—
I carry them the same way light carries water

Dusk is an ending I can wrap myself in

and of course what I mean is that
I am small and tomorrow can only be
a beginning

When you have to shoot the horse

it rained somewhere today
but it did not rain here

dust tells one single story:
what is no longer

the leather continues to patina
and all the gates are shut

footprints lead out to the wood
just beyond the pasture

the return set have yet to be pressed
and dusk is beginning to purple

it will rain somewhere tomorrow
and that place will be here

any tiny canyons can be smoothed over
and filled. the wood will be unchanged—

it'll be as still as it was yesterday
though only the quiet will echo

After

Do we come back with our hands—how I would love to hold you again,
after.

Can you see its ending?

- this rain
- these leaning (resting) flowers on the table
- that gifted book, dog-eared, scribbled in
- the shadow your still body casts
- a prairie's breath
- your collarbones
- this sound, its howl, its longing
- (by that I of course mean speaking your name)
- gentleness, its fluttering, how it keeps track of nothing
- leaving and its echo
- the day playing on repeat as I try to sleep
- *this life we have pieced together, undone, and set together again
- (so, so many times)

*no, I don't think that one has an end

I'm sorry I never call

so much of me is still a young child
frightened in the sharp dark, calling out

your name

how do we carry this

guilt of knowing they did not know how to love well
and yet, they tried so very hard

Breeze

we weren't meant to be
and yet we were
            cleaved apart

still sitting here
in your sunlit hillside
            there is no

breeze

I'll leave a light on for you

In order to pluck the ripest, least-grasped fruit,
I'll stand on the tips of my toes on uneven soil.
My best dreams are you untethered in a sunbeam,
your face drunk with light, your name a song
the wind knows by heart.

When I say I'll leave the light on for you,
what I mean is I have colored you into the oil painting of my life.
We are now a museum of tenderness for onlookers
to be amused by. We are still because we want to be.

It means I don't consider your
departure—I don't think about the light switching off.

Lavender Town

A dark porch. The coin-sized moon.
Silhouettes of trees, their neon-lined
canopy. This unforgiving hour.
This is what is called living.
Being in places we haven't been alone.

Strawberry

Watch as I open like a door
or a pair of hands unwrapping a new prayer.

Sometimes, it is better to shift through the wall
like a ghost newly excited about haunting.

My only lament is that I should've wanted more—
not more as in more but *more*.

You, yes, but also your hands; not just the light, no,
but the light you softened by pressing into it.

And also the air was sweet when you walked through it.
I wrote about a strawberry—about you eating a strawberry.

When you're not here, I make you here.
Beneath the tall oak, your shadow lays its head in my lap.

The problem is when there is nothing, there is also
everything—I want to write about tomorrow, but

I can't unless it's you opening its door.
I write about your hand on the doorknob—

I write about you opening the door.

I could say

I have wasted this life—
the shrewdness of neon lights, of
your fingers in my mouth, the
countries we build with our hands
that we say can't be lost, and yet
we eventually forget how to return
to them.

The conversation I had with my dad that changed me:

Instruction manual on caring

You empty. Then a little more
more—if you can handle it.
Watch the sun saunter across
the high points of the sky,
feel the shadows it leaves,
offer them what is left of you,
leave a jewel on their tongue.
When someone recites your
name like a prayer, clasp
their face in your palms as
though you're plucking a peach,
perfectly ripened, off the
branch. Someone is always loving
you—even when you're
all alone. Though it is impossible to
witness if you've turned away
from yourself, that is to say if
you become empty and do not let
someone unravel you.

Imagination

each time something is in my hands
I must consider a reality in which it is not

Together

We lie in our bed—a lovely field.
Us and the air. The air being made sweet
by us being there. We are still, and
the wind doesn't exhale too loudly
as not to disturb. There is lightning
somewhere, probably,
but not here, as it is not needed.
We see by feeling with our hands.
So we do not need light.
We hardly need the
air in our lungs,
just our
hands.

A flower blossoms each time you breathe

My favorite color is you speaking my name
early on a December day.

The smoke of your breath a blanket, a prism—
I see countless todays in this mirror.

Tomorrow is a wish the wind carries;
when you're far enough away that I cannot hear your voice, it is all I listen to.

Too many places can be homes; most homes are not here.
There is a heaven in your body that moves your bones.

Let us count the gaps between our breaths until we reach infinity.
When you are no longer here, the wind will remember you—

it'll carry your name like the gold in fire,
touching it and not, a moon against still water.

Landscapes

God calls pain a beginning
so I pick wildflowers for my wife.
Not as a gesture of cleansing
what I have undoubtedly soiled
but more as a letter—
inviting her, again, into
my failures that I have named
love.

Something to remember

in the thick air of late summer, you can
sit under the stars and just see light

a passing airplane doesn't need to be
someone leaving or arriving

you can be in the middle of it all
not imagining how things fade away

Sometimes partial

We are undone by our loves
and it is only those same loves
that can piece us together again

Disassociation

When I ask you to touch me,
I am asking to be unripened.

Unwrap my unblemished sweetness.
I am aging so quickly—

I can feel myself leaving again.
Tell me that what I am is still here.

Conundrum

everything is halved—
yes, there is day but have you met its moon

the sea has a body that can't hold
anything without smothering it

I see myself in its open mouth

My daughter holds a strawberry in each hand

even knowing so little
—not understanding that rain is
a gift—she somehow knows enough
to hold on to these small,
sweet things as long as she
can

I made it home in time

I'm so alive; the rivers inside me are raging

Waiting things

Our little loves frolic in the prairie of their lives—
concrete and a vastness of small, intricate things
and we, we protect them—we guide them.
No—don't step there, you don't know what is
out there lying waiting in the dark.
But we know; we love these little loves so well
because we know. The hands of those waiting
things are the first hands we ever held.

What of love is not a burden

In another room,
my wife holds our daughter—
singing and swaying
in the thickening twilight,
one reassuring the other.

A flame teaching a spark to ignite.

Oil painting

it is fall now
and the sky is growing
shorter—
I would happily let
it fall on me
if not for this afternoon
and the way it is painting
your shadow
onto me

I breathe in many colors

Orange as late-evening streetlights
lining the busy streets of downtown,
pushing against the vibrant green,
purple, and red illuminated signs.
I, too, have room for more—
if it were a different time on a different day
I would wish to be here now.
I wish I believed that conviction.
My wife's gentle, scraping steps
beside me; her seasonal auburn hair burning
beneath the glow; our daughter's eyes
brightening in the palm of her belly;
the deep purple horizon
seeping through the sieve of night
into a smooth blackness.
I believe power is a soft hand holding
a profound object—much like an infant
grasping at air, newly aware of its hands
grabbing at everything and feeling nothing
all at once.

No moon like the one we weep beneath

we are fragile creatures—
even the smallest gentle word
can hold us together

It is once again that point in a Midwest summer

in which everything starts to look like an oil painting—
each thing once stable now surreal.

The coneflower thickening like tall lavender-dusk clouds
tucking themselves in beneath the chin of the moon,

each neon sign lining the street a tiny eternity—
I press my palms into the light and ask how it softens.

Yes, I have fears. Sometimes they hold my hand while I sleep,
sometimes I wake up with their rivers still running in my palm.

Mostly they govern me; mostly I lie in the wake of their breath,
waiting for a ripe memory, a sunburst peach, a birdsong.

I reach out to touch my mother's arm and she dismantles,
each distant thing becoming more impossible.

So much of what I adore is passing at the same rate that I am.
How I hope we can leave together—if I am able

I'll carry you.

It's always summer

and I am a clearing in the trees

—that deep, unending blackness—

and you, a moonbeam

cleaving me open

There is so much

that is miraculous.
Today—a leaf gently blew
across the sidewalk
in front of me.
I nearly stepped on it.
It was just on the cusp
of vibrancy and I thought,
My word, how close
I came to ruining this gift
for someone else.

Unearthly, like a werewolf, unbelievable

after Neil Young's description of Kurt Cobain's final note on MTV Unplugged

I consider all that's gained and lost
in a single day.

So much is unraveled only to be restrung
together in fabulously uncertain ways.

My daughter stops pointing at every flower
we pass; perhaps their wonder

has grown stale. Instead, she glares ahead
absently, humming, singing

in a language unknown. But there is a
thread there to be pulled.

Her small voice rising and falling, as much
as it can, watching the birds

watch her. Singing only because she is here,
and even without the proper words

we have no choice but to worship
what we love but don't

understand why.

September

September always arrives like the stillness
after a storm.
The cicadas quiet;
the water lingering in the air unfolds into rain;
the tall summer clouds flatten
and place their palms to the earth.
And I lie down and count all the ways
in which love has gifted me
everything.

I don't have the right words for this

Autumn slowly opens the door
to find my wife hoisting up my daughter
so that she can pick an apple from the tree

You must

love it all—

what you were given

and also what was

taken.

Sometimes, when it is

quiet,

you can even have it

again.

Tourniquet

The only unavoidable wars are those fought against yourself.
I do not have scars, I have triumphs.

Acknowledgments

Thank you to the literary journals that have published previous versions of these poems:

Lamp Lit: "Hierarchy of longing"
miniMAG: "We make music while the world is dismantled around us"
Vellichor Literary: "It is once again that point in a Midwest summer"
Turning Leaf Journal: "I can't explain the state that I'm in—the state of my heart"
MudRoom: "When you have to shoot the horse"
Button Poetry: "Conundrum"
Les Hommes Publics: "What is there to worry about," "Breeze," "It's always summer," "You must," "It's possible all we have is this moment," and "I made it home in time"

William Bortz is a poet from the Midwest. He is the author of *Many Small Hungerings* and *The Grief We're Given*. You can find his work published online in *Turning Leaf Journal, Button Poetry, Okay Donkey, MudRoom*, and others. William is a music enthusiast, basketball lover, and grateful father and husband.